52 *Lessons* on
Communicating Love

52 *Lessons* on
Communicating Love

Dr. Ruth K. Westheimer

**Tips, Anecdotes, and Advice
for Connecting with the One You Love
from America's Leading Relationship Therapist**

with *Pierre Lehu*

Blue Mountain Press™
Boulder, Colorado

Photograph of Dr. Ruth K. Westheimer by Steve Friedman.

Library of Congress Catalog Card Number: 2004008383
ISBN: 0-88396-696-4

Certain trademarks are used under license.
BLUE MOUNTAIN PRESS is registered in U.S. Patent and Trademark Office.

Printed in the United States of America.
First Printing: 2004

 This book is printed on recycled paper.

This book is printed on fine quality, laid embossed, 80 lb. paper. This paper has been specially produced to be acid free (neutral pH) and contains no groundwood or unbleached pulp. It conforms with all the requirements of the American National Standards Institute, Inc., so as to ensure that this book will last and be enjoyed by future generations.

Library of Congress Cataloging-in-Publication Data

Westheimer, Ruth K. (Ruth Karola), 1928-
52 lessons on communicating love: tips, anecdotes, and advice for connecting with the one you love from America's leading relationship therapist / Ruth K. Westheimer; with Pierre Lehu.
    p. cm.
  ISBN 0-88396-696-4 (softcover : alk. paper)
1. Communication in marriage. 2. Man-woman relationships. 3. Couples—Psychology. 4. Love.
I. Title: Fifty-two lessons on communicating love. II. Lehu, Pierre A. III. Title.

HQ734.W4913 2004
306.7—dc22

2004008383

Blue Mountain Arts, Inc.

P.O. Box 4549, Boulder, Colorado 80306

*To my entire family and all my many friends,
with gratefulness.*

CONTENTS

Enjoy happiness with the one you love,
all the fleeting days of life
that have been granted to you
under the sun.

— Ecclesiastes 9:9

52 Lessons on Communicating Love

Introduction

Every second that we are around other people, we are communicating, if not with our voices, then with our demeanor and body language. But if you don't pay attention to what you are "saying," you may send out the wrong message. That is especially true when it comes to your romantic partner. It's so easy to take each other for granted that of all the communication that takes place between you, perhaps only a small fraction, or even none at all, communicates your love for each other.

Now I never studied physics, but I do know something about the term "inertia." Basically, inertia means that if a body is at rest, it will take more energy to get it moving. This principle can also be applied to a relationship. If you have not been taking an active role in your relationship, it will take more energy to get it going than if you'd been regularly filling it with energy. A relationship isn't like Grandma's silver that you take out of its box once a year to polish. It's something that needs constant spiffying up.

Okay, given your busy lives, constant is an exaggeration. But how about giving your relationship a shining for fifteen or twenty minutes once a week? That sounds reasonable, doesn't it? And what do you use for polish? The contents of this book.

It's not by chance that I chose fifty-two different lessons. I want the two of you to take out this book once a week, read one of the lessons I've written together, and discuss it. By doing this every single week for a year, without fail, you'll be able to keep the inertial forces acting on your relationship at bay. If you can find the time, then by all means continue the discussion at other times during the week. Just remember, this isn't a debate where one of you is trying to beat the other. Acting cooperatively and reaching compromises is what your relationship needs, not conflict.

And don't be afraid to show a little daring. With this book, I took a chance by trying to set down some of my thoughts in a poetic fashion that includes anecdotes and important tips. Now you must show some daring by trying this new approach to improving your relationship. It's easy to make excuses, but if you don't make these improvements, you may find it a lot harder on yourselves in the end.

Of course, if your discussions are very productive, you might even be able to impart quite a lot of energy to your relationship so that it's literally glowing. But I don't want to set you up with expectations that you might not be able to meet. This is a modest little book with modest goals, but ones that you can definitely achieve.

Remember, the goal isn't to find the right answer, but merely to keep the flow of meaningful conversation going between the two of you on a regular basis. If this book can help you to stay connected, then it will have done its job.

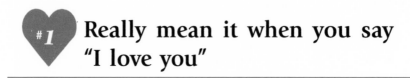

Really mean it when you say "I love you"

As the song said, love is all around us.
But while there may be hearts beating out their tunes
of love all around you,
deciphering the rhythms can be oh-so difficult.
And nothing makes us quite so tongue-tied
as putting our feelings into words.

Emotions are meant to be felt,
heartstrings to be tugged,
shoulders to be caressed,
lips to be kissed.
Our brains, our personal computers,
can process just so much.
So when feelings are running high,
be careful that the words don't get in the way.

One stumbling block to communicating love is that the very word "love" has so many meanings. Saying "I love you" to your partner is a world apart from announcing "I love Rocky Road" at the ice-cream parlor. Your heartstrings are not pulled the same way by your lover as they are by your children. The love you feel for one of your children is unlike the love you feel for another one of your children or for your grandchild. And then there's love of God, of country, and of thy neighbor.

With such a cloud of meanings surrounding this small word, it's no wonder that making our feelings known can be such a difficult task.

Tip:

One way to make the word "love" stand for romantic love is to qualify it with a two-letter word: "in." When you say you're "in love" with someone, it means more than simply saying you love them. So if you really want to be clear to your partner, every once in a while, tell them or write to them that you're "in love" with them. You could even say "I'm so in love with you." That two-letter qualifier will mean a lot to them.

Make sure your words and your actions are in sync

Sometimes words get in the way.
Sometimes they don't say enough.
Sometimes they get stuck in the back of your throat.
But just because your tongue is tied
doesn't mean you're cut off from each other.

It's great to say those magical three words, "I love you," but there are many other ways to let your loved one know how you feel.

You can say an awful lot with a look, a touch, a smile, a frown, a thoughtful gesture, a shrug, a favorite meal, a changed diaper, a silently paid bill, a remembered anniversary, or a bouquet of flowers.

You can also communicate negative thoughts in these silent ways, like leaving your dirty socks on the floor or not calling to say you'll be home late. Sometimes such thoughtlessness is only carelessness, though even then there's an unspoken message.

So let your loved know how you feel, what's in your heart, and what's on your mind... in words and in gestures.

Tip:

If you're careful how you choose your words, be just as careful in the gestures that you make. Just because nobody hears the tree falling in your forest of love, the effect of the thud will still be felt.

Tied tongues will get you nowhere... you've got to talk to each other

Two people
Lovers
Their bodies one
Night after night
And yet
Their thoughts
Locked inside
Unable to get past
Their tied tongues

Why is it that saying simple words can be so difficult? How intimate do you have to be to speak honestly with each other?

Maybe the hurdle is bigger than it appears. Perhaps each is waiting for the other to start, and then the words will come tumbling out, helter-skelter.

The key, then, is to begin. You can't unravel a knot just by pulling at it. That just makes it tighter. You have to trace the strings back to their beginnings and pull them apart carefully. You can't get frustrated if you hit a dead end. You need patience and understanding.

If the words are really stuck, you might want to try writing them out first. At least a written note can be edited before it's sent, and it will provide a road map for that conversation whenever it does begin.

It's important not to let angry words tighten the knot. To loosen conversation, you have to be relaxed. A glass of wine might help, but not more. And try not to express more than one thought at a time or your partner may get confused.

If your tongues have been tied for a long time, expect it to take a few attempts to air out what needs to be said. And never assume that a person of few words isn't always thinking furiously. Our minds never stop, and even the most tongue-tied person has a stream of thoughts always flowing across the ticker tape of his or her brain.

Most important of all, be sure to listen. Two torrents of words will only deafen you. So after you've spoken one thought, take a deep breath, and let your ears do their job.

Tip:

If you can figure out a way to enter the other person's stream of thought, you might be able to help them let go of a flood of words. This could be as easy as posing a simple question, like "Hey, what's on your mind?" But even if the other person doesn't open up, recognize that whatever you say will enter his or her thoughts and trigger reactions, so you have to choose your words just as carefully when addressing someone who answers with a word or two as someone who is a motor-mouth.

#4 Keep it simple... don't try to analyze everything

Love is like that coat of many colors.
You put it on and bathe in its glow.
You don't have to understand anything.
You don't have to see how the pieces fit.
They just do...
for the two of you.

There are men who enjoy complexity. To them, life is like a giant puzzle they're itching to solve, and the more pieces, the better. That's fine when they're building something in their workshops, tinkering with their cars, or driving to some unknown destination, but it doesn't always work so well when assembling a true love.

Love is complex all by itself. It's not an emotion that can readily be understood. You can't take it apart to analyze it. It doesn't get any clearer when seen through a microscope.

Just because love exists doesn't mean that it can be understood. So accept love's simplicity. Appreciate it without an examination. Accept it as it is. Accept each other and your singular love.

Tip:

Miscommunications happen between people, even when they've been married for decades. Don't take your partner to task for not understanding you, or he or she may withdraw into a shell. Anyone who is scolded constantly will use any possible avoidance mechanism to stop it from happening again.

If you want to encourage conversation, offer words of encouragement instead, which will oil the machinery of communication.

#5 Be sure you're saying what you really mean

Love's meanings may come in a broad array,
but one stands head and shoulders above the rest.
That's when those four golden letters convey
the feelings two adult hearts beat out for each other.

But romantic love blossoms in a rainbow of colors
that changes hues every minute of every hour.
So when you say "I love you" to each other,
take care to sense the words' real meaning.

If the person saying "I love you" can't quite define the shading of those words, then how many interpretations can the person hearing them make?

Suppose your partner is eating a super-sized burger and fries. You make a nasty comment, but you're not trying to be nasty. You're trying to say, "I love you and I don't want you to die from clogged arteries so I have to live the rest of my life without you." But does your partner understand the real meaning? Or does your partner just think you're being nasty?

You could have said, "I love you and I don't want you to die, so please don't finish all those fries." But you didn't. Maybe you didn't want to sound trite. After all, if you say "I love you" enough times, it can dilute the strength of those words. Or maybe you were feeling anger as well as love. Anger can be so strong that it overwhelms love, but while anger will dissipate, the love will always remain. So the comments you make really are statements of love, even if the other person doesn't realize it... ever.

So how do you say "I love you" when you're angry? Or hurt? Or sad?

The trick is to first take a deep breath. Words you blurt out are often words you'd like to stuff back in. By taking a deep breath, you give yourself time to regain your self-control. Maybe you'll find a different way of saying what you feel or maybe you'll decide not to say it at all — at least not while you're angry.

Tip:

I often give the advice not to talk about bedroom issues in the bedroom. The same applies for other issues that may cause a strong emotional reaction, such as raising the issue of what foods to eat in a restaurant when the person is starving and surrounded by the sights and smells of food. In that situation, allow your partner to order what he or she wants, and then have that talk with them at another time.

13

It's great to reach for the stars... just don't be disappointed if you only get as far as the moon

*Love that detonates like an exploding star
can disappear into the cosmos just as quickly.
Love that grows slowly may never burn
quite as brightly as a supernova,
but it may deliver more energy over the long run.
Remember: It only takes a little spark
to start a raging forest fire.*

Many people are out there searching for their perfect soul mates. They may not know exactly what a soul mate is, but they think they'll recognize the right person when he or she comes along.

Perfection is a wonderful goal. Always settling for second-best can lead to a lifetime of disappointment. But since nobody is perfect, you could spend a lifetime searching and wind up getting nowhere.

So you find a partner. Maybe he or she isn't perfect or the one you pictured as your "soul mate," but there is definitely some chemical reaction going on between you or you wouldn't be together. Could it bubble and boil more strongly? Perhaps. Would that chemical reaction be stronger with someone else? Maybe. But don't be too quick to abandon a relationship because your partner doesn't fit the definition of "soul mate."

The French call that feeling of instantaneous love *le coup de foudre*, the lightning bolt. Luckily, the odds of being hit by real lightning are small. Maybe unluckily, the odds of being hit by *le coup de foudre* are also small, but at least it's not the only way to find true love.

Tip:

We live in a world of instant gratification, and that often means we end up being less satisfied. Fast food doesn't compare to a meal that took hours to prepare. Ready-to-wear clothes never fit as well as those that are hand tailored. So just because a relationship takes some work on the parts of both people to come together, it doesn't mean that it is filled with any less passion than one that sparked at a first glance. In the long run, it may actually provide a lot more heat than a relationship that starts off quickly but then peters out just as fast as it began.

Don't take your partner's foibles personally

Why does he always forget his keys?
Why can't she be on time?
These are questions you could ask yourself
until the end of time
and never get an answer.

We all have our good points,
but they're paired with the bad ones.
Without that mix, we'd be boring.
With it, we can be taxing.
What makes it all worthwhile
is the love we share.

Your partner's foibles do not exist solely for the purpose of driving you crazy. This is one part of being in a relationship that can be quite hard to accept.

In all likelihood, each foible was part of your partner long before you met. It's not something that he or she does to make you upset. It's just something that he or she does.

So don't take foibles personally. It won't make them go away, and it will drive you crazy. Foibles must be accepted the same way that you accept that beauty mark on her chin or that bump on his nose.

Tip:

Some foibles are too annoying to put up with, and you have to find a solution, aside from the obvious one of getting the other person to stop. For example, if your partner's snoring keeps you awake, you may never be able to get him or her to stop, but you could sleep in separate bedrooms.

#8 Romance is more important than you may think

In order for love to thrive, not just survive,
it needs a protective environment.
We call it romance,
and it is as necessary to love
as the air we breathe is to living.
Love can't exist in a vacuum.
It needs more than two individuals
staring blankly at each other.
For love to grow, the two people need to communicate.
The sounds, smells, sights, and touches
that are the main ingredients of love
must somehow be passed back and forth
between the lovers.
Romance is the medium
for this transferal.

Some people think romance is corny. It's not — it's necessary. Others, especially some men, think romance is somehow demeaning. But being romantic doesn't make a man less of a man. It makes him more of one.

Love can be hard to put into words, but in the form of a bouquet of flowers, it can never be misunderstood. Love in the form of taking on some household chore can't be miscommunicated. Love that is accompanied by the words "I'm sorry" will never be rejected. Love in the form of focusing your total attention on your partner for a few minutes or a few hours, even when there's something else you'd rather be doing, will speak volumes.

Tip:

Some people are confused about romance and think it can be bought. While money may be able to help create a romantic atmosphere, romance itself doesn't ever have a price tag attached to it, nor can it be wrapped in a box from Tiffany's. It just needs to be a significant part of you: a thought, a block of time, a sympathetic ear, some warm arms, the pressure of a back rub, the flutter of a kiss. Love needs to nestle in the cocoon of romance. You don't need threads of gold or silver to weave your own safe haven for love. All that's required is a small part of yourself.

#9 Play your song

Remember your song?
The one the band played at your wedding?
Or the car radio blasted on your way to the beach?
Or the violinist serenaded you with at
your favorite Italian restaurant?
Of all the sounds that fill the air,
piercing through the cacophony of life,
this tune provides the two of you
with the most joyous noise of all.

If love requires occasional peace and quiet to prosper, it can also thrive surrounded by some joyous noise.

Don't allow your song to disappear into the ether. Use it to communicate the love you have for each other; maybe even play it every day.

Perhaps you could use it to wake up to every morning or listen to it right before you go to bed. Use it as the background of your voicemail. Whistle it while you're preparing dinner.

Others may share your song, but when you set the music playing, for that moment it's all yours — not just for one of you, but for both of you. The notes can help tie you closer together, and the more you play it, the tighter the ties that bind will be.

Tip:

While music is meant to be heard, it can also be written down in notes. There's a woman in Montreal who makes pins out of the music of popular songs. Whether it is one of her pieces of jewelry or in another form, like stationery, you can show your love for your song and your love by displaying these notes in a variety of places where sounds are out of place.

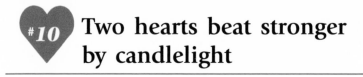

#10 Two hearts beat stronger by candlelight

*Candles not only provide light,
but also shadows
that move along the walls
and trigger your imagination.
When bathed in candlelight,
you can be anywhere
and anyone you choose.*

When cavemen and women walked the Earth, the dark was something to be feared. They tamed fire and the night was pushed outside their caves. Huddling around the fire, they found safety, warmth, and pleasure.

Today we have little contact with fire. Our homes light up and our food can be cooked without any flames at all. Yet our ancient love of fire remains. Instinctively we are attracted to a flame, not only for its wavering beauty but because a loved one basking in firelight's soft, warm glow emits a special magnetism. That's why two hearts outlined by the radiance of a flame beat just a little faster.

Fireplaces are great for reconnecting to the crackle and pop of a raging blaze, but a flame can also be cradled in a much smaller frame: a candle.

Candlelight nurtures romance. Its soft luminescence encourages loving gazes, whispered words, delicate touches, and sensual stirrings.

Tip:

Candles work best in groupings, which can be arranged to provide the utmost in atmosphere. They can be gathered together or spread around the room. It's not really important how you arrange them, but the process itself will put you in a romantic mood. When you're done, you and your partner can settle into your private cave constructed of darkness and light.

#11 Turn off the TV... turn on the love

*Some noise is unavoidable.
Some is even desirable.
But if you never get a chance
to listen to your soul,
then you start to lose contact
with yourself.
And if you surround yourself
in a cloud of noise,
then you can easily lose sight
of your lover.*

In the twenty-first century, something else love needs is quiet. We live amid constant noise. Radios blare. TVs form a continuous backdrop. Ringing phones, buzzing doors, and roaring jet planes interrupt our days, while car alarms haunt our nights. All these sounds can drown out the pitter-patter of love's heartbeats.

If you never give your full attention to your lover because you're never out of earshot of some distracting noise, then you start to lose contact with him or her. You may not be able to force your neighbor to shut off his lawn mower or leaf blower, but there is plenty of noise-making machinery around your house that you do control. Even music, which we all love, can make it harder for the two of you to communicate if it's always playing in the background.

So give your ears a rest once in a while, spend some quiet time together, and feel your love grow.

Tip:

There's noise and then there's the TV, which combines sound with equally distracting images. Watching television should be done at certain times when there's something you want to watch. Keeping it on as a background to your life will only make your life less well-lived. And never put a TV in your bedroom. It's a surefire way of killing opportunity after opportunity for romance.

#12 # Look your partner in the eyes

Maybe that's how it began.
You were across the room
and your eyes met.

Soon you communicated with words
and with your bodies,
but it was your eyes that made
the first contact.

Eye contact is vital in every relationship. When spoken into space, the words "I love you" lose half their meaning — maybe even all of it. (Unless you're on the phone, of course.) It's when you say those words while looking into your lover's eyes that they mean the most.

Your eyes can express feelings that words cannot. When your eyes say "I missed you," "I adore you," "I'm angry with you," or "I trust you," your partner knows how you really feel with or without words. And when you use your eyes with your words, they add an emphasis that can't be missed.

So try to spend some time each day looking into each other's eyes. You'll be expressing yourselves in a way that words cannot duplicate.

Tip:

If your partner can't look you in the eyes, there's another type of message being communicated. Don't ignore such a sign, but try to get to the bottom of it. The earlier you spot trouble in a relationship and make repairs, the easier it will be.

Call each other by name

Dear... Honey... Snookums...
Baby... Lover... Kid... Sweetheart...
They are all endearments.
They show you care, especially when
your lover saves them just for you.
But they're not the same
as saying someone's name.

Your lover's name is more than a word. When you say his or her name aloud or in your head, it evokes everything — all your memories, all the time you've spent together, all the trips you've made, the children you've had, and the obstacles you've overcome.

Some people only say their partner's name when they're angry, they want something, or they're yelling or complaining. The name loses its valuable identity and becomes associated with negative feelings.

So make sure you use your lover's name with tenderness, caring, and emotion as often as you can. Each time you say it that way, you'll be filled with love.

Tip:

Some parents call each other Mom and Dad, imitating their children. This may sound cute, but it removes your individuality and replaces it with a role. So it's better to reserve those titles for your children's use.

#14 Your wardrobe says a lot about you

*They used to say that clothes made the man,
but not everyone believes that anymore.
People may dress up when going out,
but the home front can be a sore for
sighted eyes.*

Sure, you want to be comfortable at home. Who wants to think about what to wear when no one can see you? No one except your lover, that is.

Clothes that are holey, frayed, billowing, bulging, or hanging aren't sexy. Instead of wearing comfortable clothes that are worn and boring, try to find some that are stylish and sexy.

And while you're at it, just because you're under the covers, it doesn't mean that you're invisible. Flannel may be warm and fuzzy, but it's not romantic — especially if there are layers upon layers of it.

You don't want to be chilly, but you also don't want to be unavailable. What you wear gives many messages, so be careful what you say when you climb into bed.

Tip:

You may have some new clothes that you're saving because they're too good to wear every day. Since you can never tell how many days you have left, and you're certainly not getting any younger, take those clothes out of their plastic bags. Put them on your back or backside where they'll do some good before they're no longer your size.

#15 Make coming home something to look forward to

*You've had a hard day at the office
or a hard day of traveling
or it's just been a hard commute.*

*The kids may have been acting up,
the washing machine may have broken down,
or the loneliness was too much.*

*Up or down, down or up, whatever the cause,
on opening the front door,
the tension could be cut with a knife.*

Coming home should be a time of relief. A man or woman's home is his or her castle. When that front door closes behind you, there's an expectation of calm and getting off the rat's treadmill for a little while.

So when that open door presents you with an out-of-control maelstrom of anger, crying, or tension, you're left with no place to go.

If the bell sounds "round one" the moment one partner enters the house, then no one should be surprised if he or she comes in swinging.

There's no question that the problems at home must be dealt with, but there needs to be a moment or two of transition before they are handed over on a red-hot cookie sheet.

So let the person coming home take a deep breath, change their work clothes, and maybe have a drink. Then give him or her the bad news or whatever else it is. He or she will be better equipped to help deal with it.

Tip:

While you may want to give partners coming home a few minutes to gather themselves, you also might want to let them know that there's a storm on the horizon. Set up some sort of signal — it could be verbal or a little sign such as an actual red flag — so that they'll know to expect something.

#16 # Dare to do things differently

Boredom saps energy, his and hers.
Picture your love as a beating red light
and boredom as a gray fog.
As the fog gets thicker and thicker,
that red light becomes harder and harder to see,
eventually disappearing into the mist altogether.
It may still be out there,
but you can no longer sense it.
It may have drifted away so far
that you'll never find it again.

As you go through life, there are danger signs everywhere: red lights and stop signs, speed bumps and blinking lights, and circles with a red line piercing their hearts.

But when it comes to a relationship, visible warning signs are few and far between. Sometimes the greatest perils come tiptoeing in sight unseen, and one of the most lethal of these sneaky assassins of ardor is boredom.

Before it drains the power of your love, sweep that gray fog of boredom aside by adding energy. In the same way the warming rays of the sun dissipate a real fog, energy can pierce the grayness of your love.

All you have to do is: converse, move, run, jump, ski, walk, go. It doesn't matter where or how. All that matters is that you do *something*. The more you do, the further away you'll push boredom, and the stronger your love will be.

Beware, too, that sometimes boredom wears a disguise. It's called routine. Routines are very necessary in life, especially when there's so much to do, but they have a serious side effect, which is boredom. The key to using routines wisely is to break them regularly. Instead of doing the expected, do the unexpected. If you always eat dinner at six, then one night a week, eat at eight or nine or ten. Every once in a while, use your fingers instead of your knife and fork. If the thought creeps into your head to throw a grape at your spouse, then do it! If you pass your hubby washing his hands at the sink, pull his pants down to his knees. Sleep on her side of the bed once in a while. Slip a $10 bill to a homeless person. Wear something unexpected to bed. Drive the long way home. Tape a morning show and watch it together at night.

Tip:

It doesn't matter what it is that you do that's different. It only matters that you do different things regularly.

#17

Schedule a date with each other

Spontaneous romantic moments
are a wonderful goal,
but so is winning the lottery,
and in some homes,
each is as likely to occur.
Lovemaking that is planned
can still soar to unexpected heights,
each segment perfectly constructed,
because you're the architect.

When both partners work at an outside job, the love nest can become the sinkhole of love. Finding time to breathe can be difficult, so the chances of love popping up like a crocus in spring are limited.

But is love really better when it sneaks up on you? Can't an hour or so be just as romantic if it is foreshadowed on your PalmPilot? In fact, planned romance has one ingredient that spontaneous love lacks — anticipation.

If you know in advance that at a particular hour you'll be staring into each other's eyes, you can interrupt your day with fantasies about those coming moments. Then by the time you're in each other's arms, the experience will be that much sweeter.

Plus, planned romance lacks one of spontaneous romance's nasty side-effects: rejection. "I'm just not in the mood" or "But it's the biggest game of the year" are excuses you won't hear when the appointed hour arrives.

So grab those spontaneous moments when they come your way, but don't count on them for building your very own love shack. Make certain that you stow away some precious hours for each other. The interest you earn waiting will be well above prime.

Tip:

While scheduling may be essential to the good health of your love life, make sure that your planning includes variety. A date for the two of you to get together that always falls at the exact same moment of the week can become boring. Make sure to add a good dose of variety to your scheduled encounters in terms not only of time, but also of place and activities.

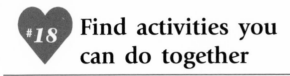

#18 Find activities you can do together

Couples who do things together
are couples who have good relationships.
If they're schussing down the slopes or
batting tennis balls across a net or
scouring the countryside for antiques or
cooking up a storm in the kitchen or
playing bridge with the neighbors or
building a house for Habitat for Humanity or
singing in a choir or
running a business together...
then you can be almost certain that
their love for each other is strong.

It's not that you must spend every minute of your lives in each other's company to have a good relationship. Every individual needs some space, but the more you bathe in each other's aura, the stronger the ties that bind will be.

Just because you're drawing breath in the same room doesn't mean that you're together. Passive time, like sleeping in the same bed, watching the same glowing TV all night, reading different sections of the same newspaper, or talking on the phone to other people, doesn't build a relationship.

To brew a strong relationship, you must mix both the quantity and the quality of the time you spend together.

Tip:

When choosing activities to do together, plan for the long haul. There will come a time when your children have left the nest and you'll want to be able to fill the time with activities you both enjoy.

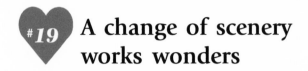

#19 A change of scenery works wonders

Whether it has one room or twenty,
your home is your castle.
But the more hours you spend inside your castle,
the more claustrophobic it can become,
and as the walls grow ever closer,
they begin to squeeze out all the love.
A breath of fresh air not only replenishes your lungs
but will inspire your romance.

If people, even lovers, are forced together long enough, yawns begin to fill the air, tempers fray, and love disappears.

When the walls start their inward march and cabin fever sets in, there's a simple prescription to restore your life and your love: a change of scenery.

It can be as simple as a walk around the block or as breathtaking as a trip around the world or anything in between. The important thing is to have a look at some new surroundings that will inspire your love. It also won't hurt if this trip involves a little exercise. If you get your physical heart pumping, the good chemical reaction such activity triggers will give a boost to your emotional heart. So even if you have to drive to reach your eventual destination, let your feet help you explore the area.

Tip:

If it's pouring outside or there's a blizzard raging, take out some pictures of a favorite vacation and use them to inspire you. Then all you have to do is open the windows, even a crack, to add some freshly oxygenated air to complete your at-home voyage.

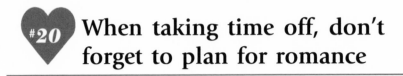

#20 When taking time off, don't forget to plan for romance

Vacations are vital;
everyone needs a break.
Tedium dulls the senses
and leaves love in its wake.

But for a vacation
to enhance romance,
you have to plan for it
well in advance.

Sharing a motel room with kids may bring you closer to your children but only increase the distance between you and your partner.

A nearby golf course may offer a swinging good time, but if it splits the two of you apart, then why bother leaving home?

If you over-indulge in food and drink, there'll be a price to pay when you push away from the table — not just on the scale but also in the bedroom.

Lying out in the sun wearing barely anything can be quite stimulating unless, of course, you burn to a crisp so physical contact is painful instead of pleasurable.

So when you're planning your next vacation, take into account the romantic factors. That way your time off will be well spent.

Tip:

Consider renting an apartment or house rather than a hotel room. You will have separate bedrooms for the children, more space to move around, and kitchen facilities so that every meal doesn't have to be in a restaurant. And the money you'll save on meals will easily make up for the added cost of the rental.

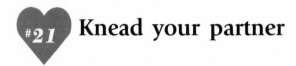 # Knead your partner

Love is all about
giving without getting,
working without pay,
feeling tired from exertion.

There's no better demonstration
of such unselfish love
as a massage.
Yet there is also satisfaction,
because you've made your partner
feel a little ecstasy.

It's not easy to give a massage. It takes a lot of energy to pound, knead, pummel, and prod your partner's flesh. Your hands may get tired and your forearms sore from giving lots of pleasure and getting nothing in return.

But your partner will be in heaven, floating on a cloud with every nerve tingling and every pore alive.

While there's nothing wrong with giving a mini-massage, where you only rub your partner's shoulders for a few minutes, try to fit in longer, more luxurious massages as regularly as you can.

And if your partner gives you massages, don't forget to give them back, if not at that moment, then soon after.

Tip:

Massages are really my only indulgence, so I can't say enough about them. If you don't have the strength to give your partner a good massage, then I suggest you send him or her to an expert now and then for a special treat. Not only will they feel great afterwards, but they may also discover some forms of massage that they particularly enjoy and can teach you how to do.

Touch as often as possible

*There are many ways of communicating —
a look, a word,
a frown, a smile.
But there's one special way that lovers share —
a touch.
Touches aren't distracting; they're supportive.
Touches shouldn't be avoided; they should be welcomed.
Touches shouldn't be held back; they should be given
whenever and wherever.*

Sure, you touch other people. You shake their hands, pat their backs, and hug when you meet. But such touches are fleeting; the space between you flows right back.

Lovers get to do so much more touching. They hold hands. They cling to each other. They stroke, caress, nuzzle, and blend into each other for a time.

As the years go by, sometimes those touches become more and more infrequent. They're reserved for certain times. Children can come between the lovers, both physically and psychologically. The kids may not like to see Mom and Dad get physical, but that doesn't mean they should dictate intimacy.

It's easy to find excuses not to touch. You're sweaty. You're reading the paper, doing the dishes, surfing the Web. But to put off touching is a mistake. Touching breaks down the barriers between two people, and the longer the time between touches, the higher and more impenetrable those barriers become.

So go out of your way to touch your partner. Make a point of it. A hug doesn't have to last forever. A cuddle can be fleeting. Every time you touch each other, you bring your psyches, as well as your bodies, closer, and that closeness is vital to the health of your relationship.

Tip:

A lack of touching is a danger signal, just like a partner not being able to look you in the eyes. If you can't break down this barrier your partner has put around himself or herself, then get help. Your partner should be enjoying touches as much as you, and if he or she isn't, then your relationship may be cracking and the two of you may soon be out of touch.

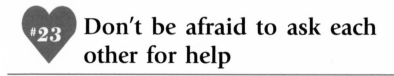

#23 Don't be afraid to ask each other for help

It can be difficult to ask for it.
You don't want to appear weak
or stupid.
You don't want to be turned down
or put down.
You don't want to be yelled at
or ignored.
You don't want to lose face
or have a face made at you.
Again.

But once you cry out for assistance
and that helping hand is next to yours,
it's such a relief
and it makes you wonder
why you waited so long
to ask.

There's no better feeling than to ask for help and be told that help is on the way. Especially if it comes with two strong hands, a wealth of expertise, a blanket of caring, and a smile.

You see, giving help is a sign of love. The person who comes to your aid is living proof that your lives are shared and that you each want to be there for the other with your time, your energy, and your knowledge.

So look at a cry for help as an opportunity to prove the strength of your love to each other. And never be afraid to ask for help — not from the one you love and who loves you.

Tip:

If you never ask for anyone's help, when you do for the first time, you may get a strange reaction. The person you're asking might not believe you at first. Don't take their attitude as rejection; it's just surprise.

#24 Take breaks during the day to communicate your love

Some days are crazy.
A ringing phone brings only dread
of the next crisis.
Romance is the furthest thing from your mind.

Then you hear his voice
or see her e-mail address,
and for a second or two,
your heart soars.
In those few seconds,
you're surrounded by love.

Coffee breaks are nice, though they may be a thing of the past. A stop at the water cooler refreshes your thirst, but not your soul. A shared lunch with co-workers adds companionship, but can leave you thirsty for more meaningful discourse.

Daytime communications between partners are important to your relationship. They can be brief and they can take different forms, but they can add moments of real satisfaction to even the worst of days.

Even if you think you're too busy to reach out to your loved one, you never are. Even a few seconds will be like a reviving splash of ice water, allowing you to slog on and make the most of the rest of the day.

Tip:

Modern methods of communication can make it easier to keep in touch, but just remember that they're not as private as words you whisper into your lover's ear. E-mails can be looked at by the powers that be, so don't say anything naughty unless you've developed some code words that allow for sweet nothings to go incognito. Cell phone conversations can be picked up by strangers, so if you're going to say something intimate, don't mention any names.

#25 Share the burdens

*$\mathcal{H}$elp doesn't have to be physical.
Sharing doesn't mean losing control.
But a loved one's support
can mean everything
in coping with life's problems.*

*So when your partner offers a lifeline
and you're tempted to toss it aside,
look into the eyes of the person
holding the other end,
and grab on.*

If you've tied the knot, officially or not, that means you're in the relationship, not only for the good times but for the bad times, too.

If you're used to going it solo, even a minor crisis may cause you to shut your psyche up tight like a clam. But if your partner loves you, he or she is going to sense that something is wrong, even without knowing what it is.

Your partner wants to help you get through this. If you lock up your feelings or refuse your partner's help, it may cause a rift. If it happens over and over again, you could drift so far apart that you lose sight of each other.

Listening to your partner's advice doesn't mean you have to take it. But by sharing your burden, you will strengthen your relationship, and that's a positive outcome no matter what started it all.

Tip:

When you offer a stranger advice, you can walk away without worrying about the outcome. When it's someone who's close to you, it may require your actual help to carry out that advice. That shouldn't deter you because if you love the person, you should want to help. But if you really can't, be careful what advice you give.

#26 **If love's flame is burning low, turn up the heat**

Remember being a kid
playing with a chemistry set?
Some experiments worked,
some fizzled.

Adults discover
that certain relationships work,
while others fail to bubble.

The secret to any chemical reaction
is putting in enough energy
for the molecules to ignite.

When two people fall in love, a chemical process bubbles up, and from their two loves an entirely new love is created.

While the two remain individuals and lead their separate lives, when they are together they're a team working as one.

Their likes and dislikes, their tastes and appetites, their desires and needs begin to fold into each other.

Soon they find themselves liking the same things, living the same lives, and loving each other more. The ingredients that went into their love melt and combine together to form a new love that is theirs alone.

When love's flame burns too low and too many hard nuggets remain floating in the brew, the couple's love may not last.

So climb into that pot, turn up the heat, and allow yourselves to melt into each other's arms, into each other's hearts, and into each other's souls.

Tip:

If too much heat is added suddenly, the mix could burn. It's better to maintain a constant flame that keeps the reaction going than to run hot and cold. That's not always possible, but whatever you do, don't let the flame die out altogether.

#27 Don't wait until you're in the mood

*In these hectic times,
with work pulling you one way
and kids pulling you another
and the wash and the garbage
sending you everywhere but the bedroom,
it can be hard to get in the mood.*

*The secret of getting in the mood
is to ignore the mood you're in
and get into that bed
together
with the phone off the hook
and the door locked!*

Editors love printing articles about sexless marriages because they know so many couples find themselves, if not in that state, near to it, so they'll rush out and buy the magazine. But the cure for not having enough sex is not reading a magazine, it's having sex.

The French have a saying, *l'appetit vient en mangeant,* which means that your appetite will come once you start eating. The same is also true of sex.

Of course, if you hate sweet potatoes and someone puts a plate of those tubers in front of you, your appetite isn't going to magically appear, unless you haven't eaten in days. But here I'm talking about getting up close and personal with your beloved. This person is never unappetizing. It's just that your thoughts and your libido have been distracted. By getting the two of you as close together as possible, the scent, touch, and warmth of your partner will quickly push those distractions out from under the covers, and your libido will take over from there.

Tip:

As important as it is to get yourselves locked into an embrace, it's equally important to avoid getting interrupted. Children are one source of potential disruption, and while you can't predict what they'll do, a simple hook-and-eye lock on your door can stop them from coming into your bedroom unannounced. As for the phone, simply take it off the hook. Give it a minute or two to stop its angry beeping, and you and your partner can then share some moments of bliss without a care in the world.

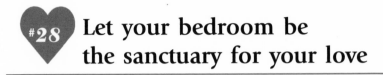

#28 Let your bedroom be the sanctuary for your love

For love to flourish,
it needs a special place
where it's not competing
for time and space.

It may feel extreme
to consider it hallowed ground,
but if your bedroom is not
the sanctuary for your love,
then where else is?

Your bedroom is the one room in your house that deserves a certain respect because it bears silent witness to and shelters your love.

If you remove all the mystery from within those four walls, you'll be weakening the fabric of the bond you're trying to build.

If the door is never shut, or if it doubles as a work room, children's playroom, exercise area, TV viewing place, or snack bar, how can opportunities arise for spontaneous signs of affection?

Try to think of your bedroom as a garden, and put up a fence to protect your little seedlings of love and give them a better chance to grow.

Tip:

If space limitations leave you no choice but to have your bedroom double as something else, then at least put some time limits on these other activities. Remember, cuddling is just as important as paying bills, and far superior to watching the evening news.

Days and nights offer two very different opportunities to share your love

As the earth revolves around the sun,
our nights turn into days,
our darkness into light.
But we now can make our own sun
or extinguish it as we like,
allowing us to share in each's delight
whenever the mood is right.

In the light,
you can stare into each other's eyes,
examine the translucence of her skin,
the tautness of his muscles,
the brightness of your smiles.

But in the dark,
you can sense each other's love,
slide over her goose bumps,
grasp unto his strength,
enter into your very souls.

Never be ashamed of what the light shows. Shame is reserved for strangers. Lovers share everything, including moles, bald spots, and cellulite. You're not naked in front of your lover; you're simply in your natural state.

But the light can also block certain senses. The vision of loveliness that is in your arms can so overwhelm you that you can't use your other senses more than tangentially. That's when curtains, blinds, or shades need to be called upon to mask the light.

If all you see are shadows, then your eyes no longer take center stage. What becomes important is the skin you touch with your finger, the wisp of hot breath on your cheek, and the whispered endearments in your ear.

Sometimes even those shadows are too much. Occasionally you may want to lock yourselves in someplace where not even one photon of light can reach you, a place so dark that you can't see anything: not your hand, not her nose, not his lips. And if you choose not to speak, then your sense of touch becomes the focal point, and you can experience your lover in a way that you might never do otherwise.

Complete darkness is also a little bit scary. You know you're alone, but there could be something else out there. So to compensate, you hold each other just a little bit tighter. You wrap that cocoon of darkness more closely around your shoulders, letting the fear within bring you even closer to the one you love.

As the two of you huddle against the invisible elements, it's a moment you want never to end because you've never quite felt this close before.

Tip:

When planning a romantic vacation, don't just think about the daytime conditions, like how much sun or snow there will be. Look for someplace that will offer you some darkness, like a little bed-and-breakfast tucked out of the way, rather than a chain hotel surrounded by bright lights. This type of getaway is likely to be quieter, and the fewer distractions, the more you can concentrate on each other.

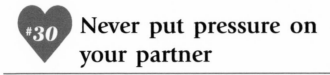

#30 Never put pressure on your partner

Jostling your way through a crowd is rude.
Tailgating can land you in jail.
Used car salesmen are too pushy.
Debt collectors are worse.

No one likes to be pressured,
particularly when it involves something pleasurable,
because it removes all the pleasure.

So a good lover knows
that it's okay to ask
but not to use pressure.

A man starts thinking of an illicit pleasure. He asks his lover if she'd like to experiment a little. She thinks about it and decides against it. That should be that. But then he keeps bringing it up. And she keeps turning him down. It may even lead to fights.

If an act is supposed to be pleasurable, it can't take place under pressure. Being forced to do something will only squeeze out any possibility of pleasure. And if any chance of pleasure is removed, why would anyone ever acquiesce to this act?

It's a Catch-22 sort of situation. But in some relationships it becomes a pit of quicksand that neither party seems to be able to escape from: not the person putting on the pressure or the person being pressured. And if enough pressure is exerted, the relationship itself can get sucked all the way down into that pit and never escape.

It's perfectly okay to ask your lover to try something new. There's nothing wrong with talking about your love life and how to make it more exciting. But at some point, if one partner has made up his or her mind, talking becomes pressuring. And if the other person keeps up the pressure, then it's not romantic, it's not sexy, and it's not nice.

Tip:

After a few months have gone by, it's acceptable to make your request again, but only if it's done with a soft touch. And if your partner does ask nicely, don't jump down his or her throat because they've raised this issue again. If they've been considerate about their request, then you owe them a considered reply.

Dr. Ruth K. Westheimer

 # Sometimes you have to compromise

Some yeses have to become no.
Some noes have to turn to yes.
Some pleasures have to be foregone.
Some have to be accepted.
Some nights have to wait till morning.
Some mornings have to imitate the night.
Some spontaneity has to become scheduled.
Some schedules have to be put off.
Some headaches have to be respected.
Some aspirin has to be taken.

All love is warm.
Some love is hot.
Two partners scorching with fever can melt into each other
without getting burned.
But each of us has differing amounts of fuel.
One person's fires may flare up more often
than his or her lover's
or with greater intensity.

These inequalities have nothing to do with the quality of a person's love. More is not better. Neither is less. They're the same, but they're different, which is a dilemma that has no answer, except that the answer is love.

Love calls for compromise. If two people can't balance on the seesaw, then one has to move closer to the center, closer to the other. But while the laws of physics control seesaws, the laws of love are not exact. There is no formula. There are no tables to consult. The two parties must figure it out for themselves: without anger, without bitterness, and with love.

The objective to always keep in sight is pleasure. The objection to always keep in mind is pain.

> ## Tip:
> If you must turn your partner down, never do it in a way that is curt or offhanded. Always let them down as softly as you can. In the long run, you'll find such kindness will pay off handsomely.

#32 Make sure you're not faking it too much

You can fake listening to each other.
You can fake a smile.
You can fake enjoying each other's company.
You can try to fake your partner
into believing empty words
or empty emotions,
but too much faking will cause damage.

The term "faking it" has certain connotations. Remember the movie *When Harry Met Sally?* There are certainly dangers to that type of faking it, and though it's okay to use that technique occasionally, it's not the only faking that people in relationships do.

No one can always be "on." Everyone gets distracted. It's all right to pretend now and again. It's okay to accept a fake response as real.

What's not okay is faking it too often — in bed or out of bed. A relationship can absorb the occasional fake. Some fakes may even strengthen the relationship, like not mentioning your partner's flab, but when faking turns to habit, it becomes difficult to tell reality from falsehood. It tears at the seams of the relationship, slowly pulling it apart.

So you can fake, you can dodge, you can weave, you can even tell a white lie — occasionally — especially when it's to keep from hurting your partner.

If you find yourself faking over and over, then it's time for a reality check. Put your license to fake at the back of the drawer, and don't take it out until a few months have passed.

Tip:

While I'm not against the occasional fake or white lie, when you use such an artifice, you must be very careful not to be transparent. Being caught faking, even if it's with good intentions, can have disastrous consequences. So never fake in an offhanded way, but carefully consider the consequences.

#33 **Exercise together if you want to become gold-medal lovers**

When boredom sets in between the sheets,
it's time to jump out of that bed
and get your motor going on the ground.

A flabby body leads to mushy lovemaking.
But if you get your heart pumping
and your circulation going,
then the two of you can become
gold-medal lovers.

Most of the time you don't think about your blood as it moves throughout your body. The one time that you might prize how your circulation works is during lovemaking. It's when your blood flows strongly "down there" that arousal mounts in your brain. And that's true for both men and women.

Not only do couch potatoes get fat, they also tend to have mediocre love lives. Your libido depends on having a vigorous physiology. If everything about you is drowsy, then your love life will be a snore, too.

I'm not a diet doctor. I'm not talking about how much you weigh. The only thing that concerns my specialty is how active you are. If you have a lot of energy, then your sex life won't suffer. But if you tire out easily, then your sex life won't be very potent.

Since I'm telling you to get more exercise to improve your love life, I'm also going to suggest that you help motivate each other by exercising together. You may have to start off slowly by simply going for nightly walks in the neighborhood. But eventually you'll be able to do a lot more. You can bike together, play tennis, go kayaking or canoeing, whatever suits your fancy. If you're both doing it, then when one of you feels like being lazy, the other can give a jump start.

Tip:

Since I'm a skier, I like to say that skiers make the best lovers. I believe skiers do make good lovers, but I know that it's not because of skiing per se but because skiers are very active and vibrant people. Now skiers don't have to go down the mountain together; they may have different levels and belong on different slopes altogether. But at the end of the day, they'll have adventures to share and a warm glow as well. So while there are times when you should exercise together, it's also okay if "together" means at the same time, but not in each other's sight.

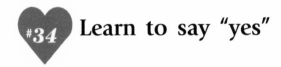

#34 Learn to say "yes"

The easiest word to say is "no."
There are rarely repercussions
when you say no.
You didn't promise anything,
so there will be nothing to regret.

But always saying no is sad
because you miss out on a lot
of what life has to offer.
You may avoid the small regrets,
only to suffer the larger one,
which is a life devoid of pleasure.

The word "no" can be very damaging to a relationship. If said over and over again, it places a barrier between the two partners. The person saying no may feel that it offers a measure of protection, but in fact, he or she is actually withdrawing into a place that is empty and cold.

I know that it can sometimes be scary to say "yes," particularly if you don't know all the possible repercussions. But it can also be very sensuous. By saying yes, you're giving yourself to the other person. You're taking a risk, which is not that risky if the other person really loves you.

In your heart you know that your lover would never hurt you. In the long run you'll probably get rewarded, but you might not realize that at the moment. Intellectually you might trust this person with your life, but emotionally, your trust might not extend to giving him or her an affirmative response that doesn't come with an ironclad contract.

Tip:

What would happen if you and your partner agreed not to say the word "no" to each other for twenty-four hours? Talk about doing this and see if you each have the courage to attempt something as daring as this. You'll each be vulnerable to the other's whims. It will be like walking on a tightrope; you'll have to count on your partner to be the safety net that keeps you from getting hurt. But it also might be enlightening and end up making your relationship stronger, particularly if one of you is usually very quick to say no.

 **If you're having problems connecting, get help now!**

Birds do it.
Bees do it.
So how come humans
have such difficulties
doing it?

VCRs are hard to program.
Computers crash regularly.
But shouldn't sex come naturally?

I'm a sex therapist. That means many of the people who come to see me in my office have some sort of difficulty with their sexual functioning. (For other clients it is the relationship that is in trouble.) Since sex is vital to human reproduction, you might think it odd that people could have a problem with it. That is until you look around and see that more than half the people around you, both young and old, need some sort of lens just to see.

Our bodies are delicate, and they don't come with an instruction manual, which is why a vast medical community has sprung up to treat the physical problems that humans encounter. So if people have problems with every other part of their anatomy, it shouldn't be surprising that they may have difficulties with sex.

What is surprising, however, is that, while most people

won't hesitate to visit a doctor to cure any other type of ailment, when it comes to sex, there's a great hesitation to do anything about it. In fact, many couples won't even talk about any sexual difficulties to each other, much less to their doctor or a sex therapist.

Despite the sexual revolution, the birth control pill, sex in the media, and Viagra, we basically remain a prudish society. Sex is something that almost every adult does, but very few talk about. And so many people have a sexual dysfunction of one sort or another and, rather than try to fix the problem, they suffer, in most cases, needlessly.

If your sex life is in need of some repairs, make an appointment with a sex therapist and see what can be done. Being sexually frustrated is not good for your relationship or your health.

Tip:

Though sex between you and your partner takes two, sometimes only one of you is willing to admit that there is a problem. Even if it's the other party that has the problem, and even if that person refuses to seek help, it's still worthwhile for you to go to a sex therapist by yourself. The therapist may be able to suggest ways of improving your sex life with your partner just by talking to you, or the therapist may be able to help you persuade your partner to make an appointment.

Dare to be like a turtle

Nothing can happen to a turtle
when it is inside its protective shell.
But the turtle cannot stay put forever.
Eventually it must stick out its neck
to search for food and a mate.
We all have a bit of the turtle in us,
wanting to stay safe and warm inside our shell.
But if we're going to get anywhere,
we must be like the turtle
and dare to stick out our necks.

Humans may not have physical shells to hide in, but we can put up psychological barriers that are just as impervious. At times, it may appear easier to hide from life, at least for a moment, but if you find yourself hiding more than coping, then this easy path may be the start of a slippery slope that you'll never climb up from.

Just as a mature turtle's shell doesn't change, a person's psychological shell also hardens over time. As years go by, it becomes more and more difficult to let the real you shine through. At first you may only want this shell to shield you from the outside world, but over time the one who loves you will also start to feel excluded. Soon your shell, donned for protection, will turn into a prison, with you in solitary confinement.

And even if you intend your shell to be your entire home, so that it includes your mate, there's a good chance that your partner in life will want to go outside: with you, if possible, without you if he or she must. Soon your home will seem like a prison to him or her, and an escape will be the only way out, leaving you behind.

So adopt the turtle as your role model. Feel free to snuggle up in your shell occasionally, but also make a point of getting outside of it every day.

Tip:

It is a scary world, and some people have a very hard time going out into it. If you feel like that shell is becoming a prison, seek out a counselor who can help you create an escape hatch.

#37 Love shouldn't be blue

Love wilts without smiles.
It droops under the weight of tears.
It grows pale when it's kept indoors.

Storms of anger can melt away as quickly as they boil up.
Feelings of sadness or anguish can be longer lasting.
An injured heart can do as much damage
to an emotion as ethereal as love
as an outraged spleen can do to all your emotions.

If you're constantly drowning under waves of blue, you must learn how to swim for shore. Depression puts your whole life in shadows and prevents you from letting your love shine through to the people you want most to see it.

It's okay to feel sad once in a while. It's part of the human condition. The death of a loved one, the end of a friendship, even the loss of a valued object can make you cry and feel miserable for a time. But eventually you do get over these blue moments. When nothing sets off your sadness and instead it's a constant shadow, then it gets another name: depression.

If you can't shake the blues by yourself, seek professional help. Remember, it's not just your life that is miserable; your constantly flowing river of tears could also be drowning your relationship. And if your partner is the one who's always down, don't just allow yourselves to drift apart because of it. If he or she can't get out of the doldrums alone or with your help, then do whatever it takes to make certain your partner gets the help he or she needs. Do it for him or her, because you love your partner, but also do it for the two of you.

Tip:

While anger boils up quickly, makes itself noticed, and then evaporates, depression sneaks in on little feet and makes itself comfortable and won't leave. Because of its quiet nature, it's easy to overlook. If you, or a loved one, are acting differently, especially if you're sleeping a lot more than usual, then don't hesitate to go to a doctor. It's better to call in a false alarm than to let depression do even more damage because it was ignored.

#38 Don't put too many bad apples in your memory sack

Some relationships spew out far more bad memories
than good ones.
The longer you stay together,
the more of them accumulate —
cluttering up your brain,
tiring out your psyche.
Your memories represent a lifetime's harvest.
Do your best to avoid putting too many
bad apples in your sack.

When you graduate from school, at the end of that last day of classes, you clean out your locker. In the spring, you might clean out your closet. Anything that doesn't fit goes right into the bag for Goodwill.

When you move to a new house, you are supposed to leave the old one swept clean. Nothing can be left behind, not even the dust bunnies in the corner. But however much you'd like to sweep through those brain cells of yours and junk the memories that cause you pain and suffering, you can't do it. Your memories are stuck there. Forever.

But you're not without recourse. While you may not be able to remove the unpleasant memories from your brain, you can try to stuff as many pleasant ones into it as possible so they overwhelm the bad ones.

For instance: You can't stop a loved one from dying. The memory of that awful day will always be distressing. But there are hundreds of good thoughts about that person stored in your memory banks. Use them to wash away the black clouds.

You and your partner may have had some bad moments. There may have been a period when you were fighting constantly. One of you may have hurt the other. Badly, even. But if you've decided to stay together, then you don't want that period of time to spoil your future together. You can't forget bad memories, but you can keep yourself from dwelling on them.

Tip:

When bad memories are shared, it's even more important that you help each other to overcome them. Just the fact that you are working as a team will make it easier. So if you and your partner have had a rough spot or two in your relationship, keep a watchful eye out for any signs that your partner is experiencing a flashback to that time. An extra hug or two, a few whispered sweet words, and a kiss might be all he or she needs to return to the present.

Repair any breaks in your relationship before it's too late

*Love should never be associated
with the word "hurt,"
but it often is.
It can hurt so much that
it can break someone's heart.*

*Heartbreak isn't always avoidable.
But it just may be repairable.*

Sometimes fate deals you a lousy hand. A lover is forced to move away, someone steals your lover's heart from you, or death cuts your heart in two with his scythe.

Avoidable heartbreaks are the most tragic. You're already together, but something is trying to pull you apart. It starts with a wound — real or perceived. An apology would cause the wound to heal, but pride or stubbornness or stupidity keeps that apology locked inside.

That one wound might not be serious, but when added to a series of others, the consequences can be fatal. So the two lovers become two haters and the love is shattered.

While the leftover cracks might not make gluing together the many pieces of a shattered mirror worthwhile, a love is not so easily replaced. If there is any chance at making a repair, even if it takes bringing in an outside craftsperson, then that's what you should do. Otherwise you may spend the rest of your life stepping on those shards of your love scattered all around your life. Each shard is labeled with a "what if?" and each is capable of causing endless pain. They can be dulled by the years, swept away by a new love, or used for endless episodes of self-pity.

The solution is to become a fortuneteller — to see into the future and realize that love needs to be put above all else. Petty emotions have to be put aside to protect the bond between the partners.

Tip:

When someone suffers a heart attack, it's obvious that every second counts and that the patient needs immediate attention. It's not as obvious to many people that the same is true for a broken heart. Too often people wait until it is too late to get help to repair their relationship. The moment to seek professional counseling is the second you see that the problem is out of control. Waiting, even days, may make any form of intervention ineffectual.

#40 Be careful not to take out your frustrations on the one you love

Sometimes anger can be held in.
Other times it can't be held back.
Like a volcano,
the hot lava of angry words just spews forth.
Like a shotgun blast,
it might hit its target
but also everything else nearby,
including people you love
and whom you don't want to feel its heat.

Do you ever get angry with yourself because you forgot to put the cell phone in your purse? Or you scratched the car, and you think, "How could I be so careless?"

If you get angry with yourself or if someone at work makes you angry or another driver ticks you off, that anger may end up being directed at the person you love. Even if the tirade of fiery words is not directed at anyone in particular, it will make those nearby uncomfortable. If that happens, an apology is in order.

As quickly as that apology comes forth, its acceptance should follow. This isn't a fight where defenses need go up. This is a case of collateral damage. Since the intent to harm wasn't there and the harm was negligible, it needs to be put aside as quickly as possible.

Tip:

If you know you have a short fuse, then try to be very careful that your anger is directed at the proper party. If a driver cuts you off, don't just curse, but let those in the car know whom you are cursing at. At least that way they'll know that you're not angry with them.

#41 "He says, she says" gets you nowhere

Anger
festers,
boils,
seethes,
and burns
everything it touches.

Communications
attempted under fire
are doomed from ever reaching
their objective —
the rational mind of your partner.

The words may come pouring out, but that doesn't mean they're understood — particularly if the mood is sour or angry.

If you have to raise your voice, you're not communicating. You may be getting something off your chest. You may need the relief. But if the other person is feeling defensive, then your message isn't getting through.

Fighting isn't necessarily bad, nor is it necessarily good. It's common enough and hopefully short-lived.

So don't worry about the occasional flare-up, but do something if the fire under the cauldron never goes out. Constant bickering wears down both parties and wears love out.

Tip:

If you're always at the boiling point, try to figure out why. You may be taking it out on your partner, but the source of your displeasure may be far from the home front. Acknowledging the reason your anger is boiling up will allow you to explain to your partner why you're in a bad mood. And if it's something your partner is doing, then try to work things out before the anger gets out of control.

#42 Learn to control your anger

*Two people living together
are going to rub each other
the wrong way now and then.
It's inevitable.
You're unique individuals.
You each have foibles, bad habits,
and annoying personality traits.
Nobody is perfect,
and nobody is perfectly accepting.*

If you can get angry with yourself, there are also going to be times when you're angry with your partner. Preventing outbursts of anger is probably impossible. Limiting the damage is what is important.

For some couples, fighting is a form of foreplay. It gets their adrenaline going and their juices flowing. Afterwards, when they make up, they feel better and their love is stronger.

For others, the fighting only brings on bad feelings that can take hours, days, or weeks to heal. The response may not always seem to be appropriate, but anger can trigger emotions from the past that magnify the emotional reaction to events in the present.

It's difficult to guess what will happen during a fight. The damage may be similar to other such disputes and can eventually be repaired. Or it could be the proverbial straw that breaks the camel's back and ends the relationship.

You can't stop anger from arising. But you can control it — at least somewhat. If you love the person in your anger's path, you owe it to that person to exert as much control as you can.

Tip:

When the furies invade your psyche, even if they can't be avoided entirely, take a deep breath before thinking or uttering that next thought. Those few seconds may take some of the edge off the emotional sword you are wielding, perhaps even enough for the blade to bounce off the other party without causing any damage.

#43 It's okay to have a few secrets

There's nothing wrong with having secrets.
Your fantasies may be better left unexplored.
Once revealed they may cause jealousy.
Locked away they can't do any harm.
But too many secrets may create walls
that block the feelings you meant to share.
The trick is deciding what to reveal
and what to keep behind the veil.

Have you given your lover an all-access pass to your past? Or are there areas that remain off-limits?

If a revelation will make you uncomfortable, then your partner may feel the same. Since you don't want to cause pain, maybe that secret should remain hidden. This is particularly true when it comes to information about former partners. What you did in private with anyone else probably should remain private. Jealousy can be a hard beast to master, but particularly so when it's being well-fed by images dragged up from the past.

But if you're hiding information to maintain control, then your love, too, is being held back. You want your partner to know who it is he or she is loving. If you keep almost everything about your past and many things about your present, too, off-limits, then you're asking someone to love only your shadow and not the real you.

The dividing line can be murky and deciding what to reveal difficult. Look into your heart to find the answer. Then make sure you follow its directions.

Tip:

Before you reveal a secret, put yourself in the place of the person to whom you are about to offer it. See if you can feel how they will react. If you think that person will be hurt, then stop those words right in their tracks.

#44 Find a balance of power

You're not Siamese twins.
You're not supposed to be identical.
Each partner has
different dreams,
assorted appetites,
various views,
and distinct desires.

You may be one couple,
but you are also
two unique individuals.
For your relationship to work
and your love to flourish,
you also must be equal partners.

Coupledom is complex, and so equality has many meanings. One partner is always stronger, smarter, sexier, or more attractive, but that doesn't mean that the other isn't also strong, smart, sexy, or attractive.

It's a balance, and once you start working together, you will find that you both become even stronger, smarter, sexier, and more attractive.

If the relationship is unbalanced or one partner tries to dominate, then the other is diminished and so is the partnership. Then both partners will lose, because as the relationship weakens, so does each partner.

So even though you'll both always be different, try to balance the power. That way you each can become stronger, and so can your love.

Tip:

Even if the two of you are unbalanced, allow your partner to handle certain areas, even if you could do a better job, and grease the way with some well-placed compliments. If you take on too much you'll end up resenting it, so learn to delegate on the home front as well as at work.

#45 Don't wait for tragedy to occur to show your love

They say that love conquers all,
but that's not really true.
Some burdens are so heavy
· that even love gives way.

Sometimes love does grow stronger
because of adversity;
sometimes you don't appreciate what you have
until you're in danger of losing it.

So don't stall.
Give it your all today —
before something goes wrong,
before you have regrets,
before you're filled with guilt.

Take it from someone who lost her entire family to the Holocaust, no matter how happy you are today, tragedy can strike at any moment. Even if you do draw together because of tragic events, it doesn't necessarily mean that the tragedy won't win out in the end.

The love you give today won't protect you from some horrible event, but it will be felt by both of you and it can never be taken away.

> ## *Tip:*
>
> If you're not the demonstrative type, don't let that stop you from sharing the feelings you have for those you love. Write them a note, or go out of your way to do something special for them. If they're close to you, they'll get the message.

#46 In times of crisis, focus on your partner

If a firestorm strikes,
no matter how terrified
or tense
or sad you are,
push aside those emotions from time to time
and focus on your partner.

Dive down, away from the flames,
into the refreshing waters of your love.
Hold on to each other
and swim a few strokes
together.

You know you can't stay down there forever.
That's true even in the good times.
You'll have to face the searing heat
of the crisis soon enough,
but if you've managed to soak in some healing love,
then not only will it be easier on you alone,
but also on you together.

Sadly, there's a crisis over the horizon — maybe even more than one. No matter how blue the skies may be today, it's going to rain on your parade at some point.

When that happens, you'll know what love is. When you desperately need a shoulder to cry on, you'll know how great it is to have one right next to you.

If the crisis thunders by quickly, the relationship will surely hold, but if it lingers — stretching ties further and further apart — a weaker couple may not make it. And in a hurricane of events, even the most solid of duos may find themselves straining to hold their partnership together.

When you're under stress, it's easy to take your partner for granted, but that may leave you blind-sided by a blow from somewhere that you least expect it.

If your relationship has never been tested by one of life's more serious curves, don't assume that you know how well your tires will stick to the road.

Tip:

In times of crisis, don't leave having some private time to chance. Make an appointment where you can be alone. Family and friends may want to crowd around you to comfort you, but it's very important that the two of you connect without being under the spotlight.

#47 Your love doesn't have to suffer when one of you is away

It can be grueling for the one that's on the road.
It can be worse for the one left behind.
It can kill a romance in so many ways.
There's the exhaustion of jet lag
and too much smiling,
the bitterness of having to stoke the home fires alone,
the tension of knowing your loved one is in the clouds,
the boredom of motel rooms and their half-empty beds,
the tastelessness of meals eaten alone,
the sadness of phone calls cut short.
The road exacts its toll.
Just make sure your love life doesn't pay the price.

When you're not together, every day away from home pulls you a little further apart. There are the suspicions that come from not knowing what the other one is doing and with whom. The temptations always seem stronger when no one can see you.

It's important that you try to stay in contact with each other, which might seem easy with the modern methods of communication, but they aren't always as effective as they could be. If you get interrupted while you're on the phone, don't forget to get back to your partner, or at least send a follow-up e-mail. Often it's the not knowing that's as damaging to your relationship as the actual distance between you.

Tip:

When the road's journey ends, make sure you take time to reconnect. Assume that some damage has been done to the relationship rather than that everything is just the same as it was before. Share some private moments and repair the damage. This is especially important if the road will come calling again soon.

Check your expectations at the door... people are not going to change

#48

Don't enter into marriage expecting
to change your spouse into
a hard worker, a neatnik, a good dresser,
a blond, a nonsmoker,
a saver, a spender,
a size smaller, a teetotaler,
a person who only has eyes for you.

If you buy a compact car, it won't turn
into an SUV overnight in your garage,
no matter how much you wish it would.

Don't expect a spouse to similarly transform
just because he or she
walked down that aisle with you.

A wedding is a wonderful day. It's a celebration of your love. It's a tying of the knot. It's the making of two lives into one. It's a contract for life.

But as wonderful as a wedding may be, it does not possess supernatural powers. The two people who get married are not going to be any different after they exchange vows than they were before.

That may seem obvious, yet it comes as a surprise to many people who believe that after they are married, they will be able to change their spouses into someone else.

Were it only so. But it's not. People don't change. They may deviate from their norm for a bit. They may say they'll do better. They may make promises. They may give it the old college try. But they won't change.

It's not because they don't want to. It's because they can't. Some traits are just hard-wired into the brain. Some bodies just won't get smaller. Some people are too addicted.

Counting on such changes happening will only lead to disappointment. So instead of thinking of your wedding day as the day your spouse becomes someone new, think of it as the day you finally accept your spouse just the way he or she already is.

Tip:

Making a change, not because you want to but because it pleases your partner, is really the ultimate sign of love. But if you tell your partner that you're going to stop smoking, for example, and then you can't, you've put your relationship at risk as well as your health. So don't make rash promises in the name of love. It won't make such promises any easier to keep, and it might make your life much tougher when you break them.

Before you tie the knot again, be sure it's what you really want to do

#49

A promise is a promise, right?
If you swore to love for life once,
why do it again?

The first answer could be: Why not?
What harm could it do?
Is it the vow itself that is
the question?
Ah, there's the rub.

You walked down the aisle together once. It was a great day; so great that it could never be repeated. And the knot you tied that day became a gnarl of attachments: kids, deeds, photo albums, possessions galore. So how could you ever part?

But if you had to do it all over again, would you? That's the question that begs answering when second or third wedding vows are on the horizon.

If the answer is "Yes," then sure, say "I do, I do, I do." If the answer is "I don't know," then don't ignore this warning sign. Your feelings for each other will have changed over the years; that's only natural. But would you describe those feelings as being love? Even if you don't hate each other, do you love one another? I'm not saying that if you're not at a point where you wouldn't hesitate to renew your marriage vows that you should split apart. Only that maybe you shouldn't ignore the state of your marriage. Talk about it. Get help, if need be. Make the needed improvements to your relationship so that the next time the question is asked, you'll both say yes.

Tip:

I was once on a cruise ship where I helped eight hundred couples renew their marriage vows, and I thought it was a wonderful event, especially as it took place on Valentine's Day. But while everyone had a great time, this was really a marketing gimmick put on by the cruise line. It's what you do for each other the other 364 days that really renews those vows and keeps the relationship on solid ground.

#50

You have to work at making your love the best it can be

Some days you may push love aside.
Other times love may push you around.
Just make certain in your heart
and in your head
that you are working in unison
when creating your canvas of love.

Since you "fall" in love, many people treat love as if it were some strange beast over which they have no control. But you have more say over your emotions than you think. Put a sad movie on the VCR and you'll cry. Dance to your favorite pop tune and your spirits will pick up. You can have a similar effect on the setting of your love dial.

While love can be overwhelming at times, or so subtle you can't tell it's there, that doesn't absolve you from honing your skills as a lover. The best lovers have the most control, not least.

Even if you're head over heels in love, you should keep some control, or you risk driving away the person you adore. There are times to go overboard and other times to bank that excess love.

And at the other extreme, if your schedule is crammed twenty-four hours a day, you can't forget that you have a partner who has needs that must be met. Sure, there are days when you can take out a loan that you promise to pay back with interest, but you can also overextend that type of credit and wind up bankrupt.

You don't need any special skills to be an artist at love. You just need to always be aware that you are a lover at heart.

Tip:

A painter mixes colors to come up with various shades. You must do the same because even love can be boring if it becomes too monotone. So some days, even if you're not feeling overly romantic, turn up the heat. Shout "I love you" across the room. Put a little more oomph into that hug. Not only will your partner appreciate your use of the brighter colors in your palette, but it will probably change your mood as well.

#51 It's the little things you do each day that will keep your love strong

Grand gestures are fun.
They can make the heart soar.
But if they only happen
once or twice a year,
what's the fun in that?

Little gestures are not as splashy.
They may even go unnoticed.
But if it weren't for the raindrops,
the oceans would soon be empty.
So let your drops of love rain down.

When people lose a partner whom they've loved dearly, it's not the grand gestures that they miss, it's the little things. It's the nightly cup of tea. It's checking that the front door is locked. It's the flowers in the vase. It's drying the dishes. It's the hugs. It's holding hands.

The little things are like the nails that hold a house together. You don't see them, but they're doing their work.

And like nails, the little things don't insert themselves without some help. Each one may not take a lot of energy, but if you put just enough energy into the little things, over time you'll build a great big love.

Tip:

You've been taught to say "thank you" for presents, but do you acknowledge the little presents your spouse gives you every day? You can never say "thank you" too many times, though most people don't say it enough.

#52 ## Make every day you're in love memorable

When you're in love,
every day should be considered memorable:
every good-morning kiss,
every hug, every caress, every cuddle.

As the years of your couplehood fly by,
you accumulate
a house full of furniture,
an attic full of old clothes,
a heart full of children,
a garage full of treasured junk,
and one mind,
shared by two people,
full of golden memories.

You're not conscious of making memories. A walk down the aisle, a period of tropical bliss, a toddler's first steps, and a family vacation may stand out, but the vast majority of your precious minutes together on earth are not so easily held onto. Can you possibly remember every shared moment? Of course not.

But while so many thousands of events can't possibly stick out in your mind, it doesn't mean that you shouldn't act like they will. Even if you can't remember every time you do something together, by putting more of yourself into each and every shared moment, they'll mean so much more to you at the time they're occurring.

Tip:

Don't kiss perfunctorily. Put more energy in your hugs. Look your partner in the eyes, and mean it when you say "I love you." At the end of the day, your memory banks may not be any fuller, but your love will be a lot richer.

Tending to the Garden of Love

Your love is like a garden,
and unless you tend to it,
you'll never reap the full rewards
that love can bring.

The ground needs to be tilled with kindness,
for if it is too hard, love's seeds can't sprout.

The seeds have to be planted with care if they
are to penetrate your lover's heart.

Love needs to be watered
with kind words and compliments.

Love must bask under the warm sun
of your undivided attention.

The weeds of pettiness and lies
must be pulled from the field of love.

The fruits of love need time to grow
and cannot be picked until they are ripe.

If you don't put the required effort
into your garden of love,
you can be certain that the weeds will invade
and your garden will yield little in the way of love.
But if you work at it,
you'll find a bumper crop of love
waiting for you to harvest
each and every day.

Heart to Heart

Communications have improved
in so many different ways.
Pocket computers carry more power
than could be imagined in olden days.

But all these electronic gizmos
don't help a romance at all,
unless you're communicating
your love when you call.

Silence is like a vacuum,
drawing in all thoughts that go by.
So protect your lover's ears;
be aware what your words imply.
Choose your words carefully;
think about what you say.
Don't fill the void with just anything,
squawking like a jay.

Make sure your emotions
aren't trapped elsewhere.
Give what you say, meaning;
speak and act with care.

Then love will sound like a trumpet
and to your words impart
the clarity of romance
as you speak heart to heart.

About the Authors

Dr. Ruth K. Westheimer is a psychosexual therapist who pioneered the field of media therapy. Born in Germany in 1928, Dr. Westheimer went to Switzerland at age ten to escape the Holocaust and to Israel at sixteen to become a member of the Haganah. She later moved to Paris to study at the Sorbonne and in 1956 immigrated to the United States. There she obtained her master's degree in sociology from the Graduate Faculty of the New School of Social Research and a doctorate of education (Ed.D.) in the Interdisciplinary Study of the Family from Columbia University Teacher's College.

Her work for Planned Parenthood led her to study human sexuality under Dr. Helen Singer Kaplan at New York Hospital-Cornell University Medical Center. She currently alternates teaching courses at Yale and Princeton and is an Adjunct Professor at N.Y.U. A fellow of the New York Academy of Medicine, she has her own private practice in New York and lectures worldwide.

Dr. Westheimer is the author of twenty-seven books. She has a syndicated newspaper column and her own web page hosted by iVillage (www.drruth.com.) She has two children and four grandchildren, and she resides in New York City.

Pierre A. Lehu has been Dr. Ruth's "Minister of Communications" for over twenty-three years and has written twelve books with her. He is married, has two children, and resides in Brooklyn, New York.